JOHN LENNON
IN CONVERSATION WITH
TONY TAYLOR

Recent publications by Dr. A.J.W. Taylor

2010: ***The prison system and its effects****: Revised and enlarged edition.* New York: Nova Science.
2009: ***Cockney Kid:*** *the Making of an Unconventional Psychologist.* (Silver Owl Press, Paekakariki, NZ).
2006: ***Justice as a basic human need****.* New York: Nova Science. Taylor, A.J.W. (Ed.).
1989: ***Disasters and disaster stress****.* New York: AMS Press.
1987: ***Antarctic Psychology****.* Wellington: Department of Scientific and Industrial Research.

Recent publications by Dr. Michael O'Leary

2014: ***Die Bibel****: Authoritative History of Dr Michael John O'Leary, the Earl of Seacliff.* (ESAW).
2012: ***ARTIST*** *– art works and words* by Michael O'Leary published (ESAW).
2012: ***Wednesday's Women****,* Literary History/PhD Thesis (Silver Owl Press).
2011: ***Fences Fall****: CD of Songs from the lyrics of Michael O'Leary* (ESAW Sounds Division).
2009: ***Magic Alex's Revenge*** *–* Novel (ESAW)
(completes the *"Dreamlander Express"* trilogy with ***Unlevel Crossings*** and ***Straight****).*

John Lennon

in conversation with

Tony Taylor

*

**Previously unpublished interviews recorded
in Wellington, June 1964
during The Beatles' tour of New Zealand**

*

**Together with details of the only reported study
of Beatlemania and brief notes of a broadcast on the topic**

*

**Plus: *The Flipside of the Ballad of John & Yoko*
by Michael O'Leary**

**Earl of Seacliff Art Workshop
Paekakariki
2015**

Thanks are due to:

Andy Neill in London and Jon Baker in Auckland for tracking down Tony Taylor to identify him as the interviewer in the press photograph reproduced on the cover.

David McGill for bringing the two Herr Doctors together.

Anne Lee for transcribing the original tape recordings of the two interviews with John Lennon at the St George Hotel in Wellington.

'The Beatles arrive in Wellington, 1964',
http://www.nzhistory.net.nz/media/photo/beatles-arrive-in-wellington-1964,
(Ministry for Culture and Heritage). Updated 7-Jan-2014
'Beatles fans at a Wellington concert',
http://www.nzhistory.net.nz/media/photo/beatles-fans-at-the-wellington-concert,
(Ministry for Culture and Heritage). Updated 7-Jan-2014
'The Beatles at the St George, Wellington',
http://www.nzhistory.net.nz/media/photo/the-beatles-at-the-st-george-wellington,
(Ministry for Culture and Heritage), updated 7-Jan-2014
[The 3 photos above were taken by Morrie Hill]
John Lennon with his book *In His Own Write*
http://diariodosbeatles.blogspot.com
The Beatles with the Pataka Māori Group
http://Wogew.blogspot.com
The Beatles' signatures
http://www.beatlebay.com
(Signed at Croydon, Surrey, April 25th, 1963)
John Lennon with his cousins from Levin
http://www.audioculture.co.nz
John Lennon meets Lynda Mathews, his cousin from Upper Hutt
http://www.radionz.co.nz

Photo of Tony Taylor by Image Services, Victoria University of Wellington
Photo of Michael O'Leary by John Girdlestone

Printed at Precise Print, Paraparaumu, NZ.

Published by:
Earl of Seacliff Art Workshop
PO Box 42
Paekakariki 5034
e-mail: pukapuka@paradise.net.nz
website: http://michaeloleary.wordpress.com
ISBN: 978-186942-153-3

4

A Preliminry Note

Dr A.J.W. (Tony) Taylor is an Emeritus Professor of Psychology at Victoria University of Wellington. He was the first professor of clinical psychology in the British Commonwealth, and is the author of over 300 publications including his memoir *Cockney Kid: the Making of an Unconventional Psychologist* (Silver Owl Press, Paekakariki, NZ: 2009). He became interested in the mass-hysteria that The Beatles generated, and used the topic in 1964 as a class-exercise to get some facts when the 'fab-four' performed in Wellington during their eight-day tour of New Zealand.

Curiosity around the 50th anniversary of the visit led him recently to search the journals for results of comparable studies that other psychologists might have made. His foray drew a blank, despite the huge social upheaval The Beatles had caused wherever they went. Disappointment encouraged him to restate the need for others to take up the study of mass-hysteria. Apart from the intrinsic value of the topic in today's manipulative world, he is still keen to validate his results with those that other researchers might obtain with fans of contemporary musical groups.

Dr Michael O'Leary is a poet, artist and novelist, who, in his 2014 autobiography *Die Bibel*, (ESAW, Paekakariki) discussed the effect that The Beatles, and particularly John Lennon, had on his own decision to become an artist in whatever form that took in his life. After gaining his PhD in literature in 2011 he worked with a number of musicians to transform his poems into songs, thus bringing his writing and artistic career full circle. In this excerpt from *Die Bibel* (p110) O'Leary describes how he felt when he heard of Lennon's death:

'I wrote *Flip Side of the Ballad of John and Yoko* 'off the cuff' the moment I heard the news that Mark Chapman had murdered John Lennon in New York City: *Que pasa New York? Que pasa New York? Hey, Hey!* The tragic event was a great shock to me and many of my generation around the world. That night I went to the Captain Cook Hotel in Dunedin and met fellow poet, Peter Olds, and held a wake for John in remembrance for all he had done for us over the years. I noted that Bob Dylan, not known for eulogizing other artists of his generation, wrote '*Roll on John*' in praise of Lennon for his 2012 album *Tempest* – you see, everyone copies me eventually!'

INTRODUCTION

Despite the impact that The Beatles made on society and the continuing legacy they left with their music, Tony Taylor's study of the mass-reaction they produced was, and still is, the only one reported by a social scientist seeking factual data. The omission left journalists, politicians, and pundits to make profound utterances with opinions not always shorn of prejudice.

In the late 1960s the editors of two academic journals bemoaned the lack of interest shown by their colleagues in the topic, and recently their successors echoed the very same complaint. Yet there is a glimmer of hope that might inspire other researchers to action, because in 2013 Stephen Fry involved three bio/medical scientists to reveal the effect of music on different bodily systems: (see http://www.youtube.com/watch?v=EVN4dShaZWk - accessed 1 August 2014).

While the matter of academic neglect has been followed up elsewhere, Michael thought the general readership would like to know more about Tony's groundbreaking study – and to mull over the modestly presented account John Lennon gave him about the emergence of The Beatles as a unique group of musicians. These interviews could be among the last never to have been previously published.

In 1964 when The Beatles played in New Zealand, they were at what can be construed as the second (and halcyon) phase of their development. The first phase lasted from 1959 to 1961. It had John Lennon linked with Paul McCartney, George Harrison and a series of drummers to entertain rowdy patrons of the less salubrious clubs in Liverpool, Newcastle and Hamburg. The second phase, from 1962 to 1964, began when Richard Starkey (aka *Ringo Starr*) joined the three mainstays to create what became known as the *Mersey beat* – the persistence, tempo and volume of which invariably brought audiences to their feet, made young women scream and young men roar their appreciation. After that the band spread its wings to become billed as the main feature of concerts in Denmark, France, the USA, Asia and Australasia.

The group's third phase lasted from 1965 to 1967. During that time it rode an unprecedented commercial and professional tsunami. At the height of its fame it accepted Royal honours – to the dismay of a few former recipients. Yet the tumultuous reaction of concert fans demanding constantly to hear the favourites began to impede their musical development, and the clamour of devotees in the street encroached on their privacy. Thereafter, The Beatles sought seclusion by making zany films and studio records rather than give concert performances.

The fourth phase was confined to a short period in 1968 when The Beatles came under the influence of psychedelic drugs and Indian mysticism. They were seeking inner truths, outer peace and purity of purpose. Their lyrics reflected existential themes and their music experimentalism. Manager Brian Epstein's death the previous year, prompted them belatedly to restructure their top-heavy managerial and business empire.

The fifth and final phase began in 1969 when John Lennon was convinced that commercialism and public adulation had snuffed out The Beatles' flame of creativity. Leadership rivalries came to the fore and contributed to the group's destruction. The musicians followed separate paths. John Lennon made several albums, and wrote what became a major peace and humanity anthem, 'Imagine'. While modulating ties with Yoko Ono, he moved on the fringe of the avant-garde in art, the 'flower-power' protest against the Vietnam War, the rising military-industrial complex, and the student revolution in the United States. In December 1980 a mentally deranged fan killed him, to the abject dismay of Beatles fans throughout the world.

As for the other Beatles, after the break-up in 1970 Paul McCartney held centre-stage by mounting new musical productions with his wife Linda and their band Wings. In 1997 he was knighted for services to music, and in 2012 he played a prominent part in the concert in London to mark Her Majesty's Queen Elizabeth the Second's Diamond Jubilee. George Harrison remained interested in Indian spiritual life, and under Ravi Shankar's guidance he became an exponent of the multi-stringed sitar. He also made solo albums and films with Monty Python. In 1999, he too was attacked by a deranged fan, but survived only to die of throat cancer two years later. Ringo Starr continued to make records and give concert appearances worldwide with his 'All-Starr Band', and to appear in films alongside Peter Sellers and other notable actors.

Today, 50 years on, it can be said that John Lennon's extraordinary life carried the hallmarks of a Shakespearean tragedy, and that The Beatles were a legendary musical and social force with an assured place in history.

After his interviews with John Lennon, which are the main feature of this book, Tony Taylor asked himself: Exactly what sort of effect did the music of this quiet, unassuming and good-humoured young man and his three friends have on their audiences? To answer this question, it might be helpful to outline Tony's original research plan here, and to mention the modifications he found necessary so as to get reliable data from which to draw conclusions.

THE RESEARCH PLAN

The idea was to observe the behavior of Beatle-fans and their counterparts, before inviting a sufficient number of both to undergo standard psychometric testing for evidence of clinical hysteria, emotional imbalance and any distinctive personality attributes. Then a few questions needed to be asked about their family backgrounds and current living circumstances to see whether they might have been as feckless and footloose as some critics had suggested.

The method

The build-up and reactions of crowds expected to gather at the airport and outside the hotel where The Beatles were staying was to be noted, and impressions recorded at a concert. An interview was sought with John Lennon to inquire about the band's formation, the type of music it developed, and the audience reactions it created. John was chosen, because he was the founder of the group and thought less likely than his companions to be flippant. Initially, the New Zealand Broadcasting Service had wanted to interview John, but it jibbed at the cost. Happily they granted Tony journalistic status and provided a technician with

8

recording apparatus - in return for which they accepted his offer to give a short radio broadcast of his impressions.

An honours class of twelve clinical psychology students was trained to identify potential participants for the study. It was to invite a substantial number of both extremes to attend the university for psychological testing. To avoid potential conflict between the groups, their sessions were to be held on different days. As another precaution against untoward events, letters of authority were obtained from the Police Commissioner, Local Traffic Superintendent, and Victoria University Vice-Chancellor to confirm the legitimacy of the enterprise.

THE OUTCOME

THE AIRPORT RECEPTION

On the appointed day the keenest of the fans had been against the reinforced wire fence at the airport from the early hours. In some places the number behind them built up until it was 30 deep. The crowd seemed to consist mostly of teenagers, with a sprinkling of the middle-aged no doubt keeping a parental eye on their youngsters. A few of the older folk said they were there to express their disdain, and others to declare their loyalties for former idols of the crowds, such as Gracie Fields, Vera Lynn, Elvis Presley or Cliff Richards. It occurred to Tony that one could determine the approximate age of people, not by carbon-dating but by idol-dating!

When the aeroplane carrying The Beatles landed, the noisy throng went wild with excitement and began to chant 'We want the Beatles'. It shouted and screamed even louder when the Liverpudlians emerged. No football supporters, nor a Royal Tour crowd, had kept up such a level of excitement for so long.

9

The Beatles arrive at Wellington Airport

THE INTERVIEW(S)

The first interview took place in the St. George Hotel in Wellington in a scrum of media journalists on the day The Beatles' arrived. The second occurred in the quietness of their hotel suite two days later, after the technician found the power-cable had been unplugged and assumed the first tape was a blank. John Lennon willingly obliged.

When the original tape became available, the technician's fears were unfounded. Now having recordings of two interviews to hand, allowed checks to be made for John Lennon's consistency of response. Not only that, but the second, coming after Tony had attended the first concert performance, enabled him to ask pertinent questions about the build-up of the audience by the two earlier bands before The Beatles appeared on stage.

In chronological order below comes the first interview with John Lennon, Tony's impressions from attending a concert, the second interview, the results of psychometric testing, and finally a discussion with conclusions that might yet stimulate other researchers to enter the fray. The presentation ends with the essence of a short broadcast talk given 'for services rendered'. Finally Michael O'Leary's poignant poem brings this publication to an appropriate end.

10

THE FIRST INTERVIEW: Tony Taylor in conversation with John Lennon at a media conference during The Beatles' visit to Wellington, New Zealand/Aotearoa on 20th June 1964.

TT: I've really got a number of curious questions to ask about you personally, and the group.

JL: I see.

TT: For example, what sort of audience do you aim at getting?

JL: Uh, well obviously kids, teenagers, you know, and they usually comprise of 80% girls so that's the audience we aim at you see. When we make records we just aim to make good records you know, we don't really consciously think, 'this will do for this age group', you know, we just make records.

TT: Now what have you in mind, what sort of words or music or beat do you feel have the success that obviously you've got?

JL: Well, uh, an up-tempo record is usually much better, much more commercial than a slower record. The slower record's got to have very much more melody and, you know, it's got to be really good, a ballad, to get through. Whereas you've got more chance with an up-tempo record, with an up-tempo number that's got a pleasant melody.

TT: By up-tempo you mean something with a pretty quick pulse, and rather loud?

JL: Well the loudness doesn't matter so much as tempo ...

TT: Tempo - the beat.

JL: Yes.

TT: What sort of words?

JL: Well normally just 'I love you', 'you love me' or 'Where's she gone?'

and 'She's back', you know. Happy ones are the best ones.

TT: Reflecting adolescent love themes in fact.

JL: Well yes, vaguely.

TT: And do you find that the same sort of thing has brought you the success with your book? [Lennon's first book, *In His Own Write*]

JL: Ah well there's nothing much about love in it but I don't aim that, it's not conscious, you know it's just - the book is mainly to make me laugh and it just so happened it was published. I'd been doing it a long time - years without any thought of having it published.

TT: Do you think you would have the same effect on your audience that you're aiming at if they were to listen to it sort of individually, rather than when they come together in a group?

JL: Do you mean if we were in a group or they were in a group?

TT: Well if they were in a group. If they were sort of in smaller groups would they have the same big gross almost hysterical reaction?

JL: Well earlier on in our career we played to much smaller crowds in smaller - you know in clubs, jazz clubs and things like that and the reactions were just as good.

TT: Yes. What accounts then for the breakthrough that you've had, from the small group, where you had a good reaction, to the big one?

JL: Well, it's a natural breakthrough. If you make a record and you've get a hit, you've got to go around different places and the more people who want to see you, the bigger halls you've got to play at, so in the end you're playing in sort of coliseums or something.

TT: Yes. Now supposing I was about to start a group, what advice would you give me to help me along the way?

JL: Pack it in. To start off, to just say 'I'm going to form a group' it never works. They tried it in Britain as well as the States - every day, somebody gets the ingredients so-called ... they think it's just a lot of gimmicks, and they get a couple of fellas that they think look right and they think they've got a group - it doesn't work.

TT: No. So the thing to do is to pack it in ...

JL: If you're just walking round and you see somebody and something happens when you're watching them, well try that, but you could never just form them.

TT: No, it's got to strike at the right moment.

JL: I think so, yeah. I'm not an authority, but that's what I think.

TT: And its taken nine years has it, to reach the peak that you have?

JL: Well we weren't trying to reach any peak at first, we were just playing, for kicks and then for money.

TT: Yes, obviously you're keeping your fingers crossed. And how long do you reckon you'll ride the crest of the wave?

JL: I don't really mind. We've had a good time. I don't care what happens now. If people still want us to appear we will, and if they don't we won't be choked. Obviously you know you have to get a bit 'oh well, you know, that's it' but we're not going to cry.

TT: you know how there's always a succession of music from rock'n'roll and beat and jazz and so on: would you hazard a guess as to what the next will be, the next thing?

JL: Well as far as I'm concerned, rock'n'roll never died, it just got a bit wet, you know, because it was forced that way ... it definitely didn't die out in Britain as we proved. Because whenever we went anywhere, without any hit records, people went mad and they were pleased that we were playing the heavy stuff. It just so happened nobody had make it. They wouldn't play it cos they were against it, you see, so I'll hazard a guess and say rock'n'roll will be with us in different forms, the same way jazz has not just died out and fizzled but just got their own following, well that's what'll happen to rock. It will always be there ... but I don't know what the next big craze will be.

TT: How would you characterise your music at the moment? What would you say it is essentially?

JL: Rock'n'roll, except that Paul and I write it.

TT: Yes, except that you do write it. Now do you feel on par, say, with Bill Haley?

JL: No, because he's really more sort of, you know. Haley's almost a jazz group when you listen to him now.

TT: When you were in your teens who were your idols?

JL: Ah, I liked Bill Haley - I never went potty on him, I just sort of vaguely liked it. But Presley was the main thing, at first, and then Little Richard. He converted me completely.

TT: And did you find that again there was roughly the same percentage of 80% girls to 20% of men in the audience?

JL: Well, for Presley, yes: but for Little Richard, no, see he was the good compromise where anybody'd watch him.

TT: Colin Fletcher, who claims to have …

JL: Got his name in the papers.

TT: Yes - well you obviously know of him - he claims to have been a member of the Holly Road gang.

JL: What's that?

TT: Oh, one of the gangs in Liverpool …

JL: Oh, Holly Road? Well yeah, there were a lot of gangs but I didn't really know them.

TT: I see. Well he argues that the great thing about the music, about the beat music that comes essentially from Liverpool, is that it's made a tremendous impact upon gangs, in that gangs are far more eager to get with the beat rather than to tear each other apart.

JL: Well that's just a sort of load of rubbish that people keep saying, you know, there might be slightly less crime in Liverpool, or sort of teenage crime … but I doubt it.

TT: You doubt it?

JL: There's always been people playing music in Liverpool and there's still been gangs and everything -

TT: Now, why do you think it is?

JL: - and I don't think it's made an iota of difference.

TT: Why do you think it is that the music and the beat comes from the sort of the western side, rather than say the eastern side or the southern?

JL: Well, when we first sort of stuck our noses outside Liverpool you know, to try and get some money somewhere else as well, we did come across little pockets of places playing the same stuff as we did, say Birmingham, or Newcastle ... we went up to Newcastle without any billing at all, nobody knew us, played to a packed house that'd be packed anyway, and they went wild. You know, this was years ago and we thought 'hello', you know we thought we were the only ones in Liverpool clinging on to the old stuff, and we bumped into quite a few people and lots of them have come out now you know, local groups that are recording.

TT: So you feel that you've made yourself as it were, without the advertising buildup that we've had here, for weeks and months almost.

JL: In certain pockets we're accepted without any records at all, in England where they've wanted to hear what we're playing anyway.

TT: Particularly then you were talking about the beat that The Beatles have, would you like to ... what is it essentially?

JL: Well, we call it rock'nroll, you know, we stick by that and its just rock'n'roll that Paul and I write, so that's what we call it. Plain old rock'n'roll, not Merseybeat or Liverpool Sound or ...

TT: And this is for a particular type of audience?

JL: Well it's mainly teenagers or early 20s that come to our shows, you know, so it's for them.

TT: And this is a worldwide reaction of teenagers to the same music is it?

JL: Yes, I think it's, well rock'n'roll's been going about ten years, it's sort of faded but it was always sort of hanging round, you know.

TT: How do you account for this particular reaction of teenagers?

JL: I don't know because that kind of music, it gets over straight away, you know, there's no messing, you know. If it's played competently it doesn't have to be played all that well. It's exciting, it makes you want to dance mainly, you know I still believe that, even though they're jumping and screaming. They would dance if we were playing for two hours, they'd stop screaming, actually.

TT: Is there a limit to the screaming, do you think?

JL: There's usually a lot of screaming because we're only on for - they only see us for short periods. We do a half hour show, you see, so they scream all through it. If we were playing three hours like we did in the old days, three sometimes four, well they'd scream for a bit at first the ones that did scream, and then they'd settle down and dance or watch, you know.

TT: Would they be happy with the scream do you think? Supposing you cut the screaming out?

JL: Well, we couldn't cut it out, we enjoy it as part of the show. People expect it.

TT: People expect it?

JL: And a lot of people can hear. It's usually older people that come out of the show saying 'We couldn't hear a thing'.

TT: And what are the essential themes of your songs, for example?

JL: As I said before usually love lost or gained, you know, there's nothing much else you can write about, unless you want to write about factories and chimneys and things.

TT: And this is the universal appeal, you think?

JL: Yes, well most people like love songs, you know.

17

TT: In your own adolescence, whom did you admire?

JL: I've already mentioned Bill Haley slightly, Elvis Presley, Little Richard, we're great fans of his. Still are. And uh lots of people. Chuck Berry and Carl Perkins, and all the old rock'n'roll kings as we called them.

TT: And roughly was there the same proportion of men to women in the audience in those days when you were a teenager as it is now?

JL: For Presley and things like that - well I'm talking about films - a lot of girls went, but there was also a good percentage of boys. A person like Little Richard there were just as many boys, if not more, than girls.

TT: Now, is this linked essentially with Merseyside rather than other parts of England?

JL: No, cos when we first began to stick our noses outside Liverpool we'd play in places where we'd just die a death. This is before we made records. They asked to play the hit parade numbers, which we never played. We had a sort of snobbish attitude towards the hit parade, and here we are now in all these hit parades but we never played hit parade material. And they'd ask us for it but you get to places like Birmingham say, Manchester, Newcastle especially I remember because nobody knew us up there and we went down a bomb. And it was wild, just like these scenes now, and we hadn't even made a record. Cos they were still sort of rock'n'roll fans definitely. There were these pockets all over England that were still wild enthusiasts for it.

TT: What happens to the gangs for example? Did this in fact, this kind of music, make any difference to gangs in Merseyside?

JL: Well these gangs that - I only ever saw about two gangs in Liverpool myself in all my life there and I don't think - if there's gonna be - there's gangs anyway you know, even if they've got a group, it's our gang's group. You know I don't think we've made much difference to teenage delinquency.

TT: Finally, what advice would you give me if I wanted to start - uh become a new Beatle or something of this kind? And what is the new kind of music that's going to come up? What do you feel about the sort of crowd hysteria, or crowd reaction to you? Do you feel it's just a passing phenomenon or what? I mean, there are ...

JL: I haven't a clue. If I knew, I'd be forming groups too. [laughter] There's no way you can tell, even though some smart people think they can. It's just a matter of throwing a couple of lads that look right together and giving them a guitar. It does not work and it's happened in England and it doesn't work.

TT: What kind of music is going to succeed after you?

JL: I don't know I think beat'll be here for quite a bit in one form or the other, for years, and it'll probably end up like jazz is now, just sort of specialist.

TT: Well thank you very much indeed, it's very kind of you.

JL: Pleasure. Good night.

PERSONAL OBSERVATIONS OF A BEATLES CONCERT

What of an actual performance? The programme was skillfully arranged in such a way that audience participation and musical tempo mounted for over two hours without a break before The Beatles came on stage for the final 25 minutes of mayhem.

First a rock'n'roll band appeared in glittering suits that reflected the different colours of the sweeping spotlights, while the lead-singer cavorted and shook in a skin-tight shiny black leather suit. The audience cheered, clapped their hands and stamped their feet enthusiastically. Then the band started another number with a slightly quicker tempo that produced a few faint screams of appreciation. The audience was now getting 'with it'. The first loud screams came about half an hour later when the hall lights were dimmed, the singer carried a red torch to his face, and his supporting group of musicians was illuminated with green ghoulish lights. However, apart from sporadic outbursts of screaming, the audience was just as noisy as might be expected at any rock concert.

After an hour, along came the second band in this non-stop performance. It increased the tempo and encouraged the audience to clap, cheer and stamp even more. Pairs of girls bobbed up and down and shrieked uncontrollably. By this time Tony felt his heart racing, and he found it difficult to concentrate sufficiently to read his pulse, even with the help of an astonished person sitting alongside whom he recruited as a timekeeper.

Pandemonium broke loose when finally The Beatles appeared. They didn't wait for silence before they started to play. Nobody could hear their words, and hardly their tunes. No matter. The band produced their characteristic beat, a rhythmic thudding sound that zoomed over, boomed over, the whole auditorium through massive amplifiers. And what was the response of the audience to their second tune? The announcement of its name was sufficient to evoke another cacophony of screams.

The Beatles seemed quite unperturbed by the frenzy, and they carried on as if nothing were amiss. In fact they increased the tempo of their music, and aroused the audience to greater heights of ecstasy. Did they mind the fans coming on to the stage? As John Lennon said later during an interview, 'Good luck to them if they can get past the guards'.

There were a few quieter moments when it was just possible to catch a few of the words and tunes, but it hardly mattered because the fans knew both by heart. It seemed as if they wanted primarily to join the huge international stream of devotees of their own generation and pay tribute to the band that encouraged them to break binding conventions.

You could catch the roars of the males as they too called for 'More! More! More! They showed that girls weren't the only ones to be affected by the music. At this point the audience was up on its feet, jumping to and fro with some trying to surge towards the stage to get alongside their idols. Were it not for the timely playing of the slow sonorous beat of the national anthem, and the full glare of house lights switched on suddenly to restore reality with 'the boys in blue', there might well have been further disruption and disturbance.

Beatles' fans at the group's Wellington Town Hall Concert

THE SECOND INTERVIEW: Tony Taylor in conversation with John Lennon in his hotel suite, after having attended a concert

TT: This is Tuesday the 22nd of June 1964 and it's the third day of The Beatles' visit to Wellington. They arrived on Sunday afternoon to a tumultuous reception and went to their hotel. I was fortunate enough to be able to witness their arrival and then to have the chance of a short interview with John Lennon at the press conference the same day. Unfortunately, the recording apparatus was defective, but I have got another chance of completing an interview with John Lennon this afternoon, by courtesy of the manager of his touring company. The

Beatles gave two performances yesterday in Wellington and they've got another two tonight before they leave tomorrow morning to go to Auckland.

TT: I think - would you like to just talk a minute there?

JL: One two three: hello, hello: testing, testing.

TT: Excellent, excellent. Let me begin by saying thank you very much over this. I can appreciate that you must be feeling damn tired.

JL: I've feel like I've been in bed for about 49 hours now.

TT: Well you deserve it anyway. Now I'm as curious as lots of other people about the way your group hangs together. What is it about the particular people involved that helps you to work together as a team? How did you come together in the beginning, for example?

JL: Well, well that's a long story. We met through school friends, you know, mutual friends. I met - I had a group in - I can't remember what year it was - and I was playing, and a boy that lived near me knew Paul at his school, and brought Paul along to see us, and then I was introduced to Paul. And we both sort of agreed that it would be a good thing if he joined the group. And he joined it. And Paul was also [inaudible] with George at the time. So a year later, he introduced George to us, and George then joined the group. Then the three of us were together, and since then we've had various drummers and things like that, but us three have always stuck together, cos we got on so well.

TT: By 'getting on so well' you mean ...?

JL: Well, it took us about two and a half years to form a complete friendship you know, from beginning to end. By the time the three of us knew each other well.

TT: And this accounts for much of the easy manner of communication when you're on the stage?

JL: Yes, I'm communicating all the time you know, we don't need to speak.

TT: And, did you have - you say you had a number of drummers with you ... Ringo's with you now.

JL: Yes, drummers used to come and go. A good drummer was harder to find than a competent guitarist or bass player.

TT: Is this because there are less people interested in drumming now?

JL: Probably. And because it takes longer to acquire a good standard of drumming than it does - I mean I think it's easier to learn how to vamp a guitar to accompany a song.

TT: I think you're being modest about it - I think the guitar is a very difficult instrument.

JL: Oh, it is to play well, but you know it's not hard to find somebody who can play fairly good and sing with it, you know. But drumming, you've got to be pretty good to back poor guitarists say, and at that time we were much worse so we needed at least a decent drummer to make it move. We could sing together, but our playing wasn't all that hot.

TT: And then you - the drummer sort of helped you consolidate as a group and then you were away?

JL: Well, we had about eight or nine drummers in all, you know, and they'd come and go, and half the time it was better to be without a drummer, you know, they were that bad, until we finally got Ringo.

TT: Uh huh. And was it at that time that you suddenly sort of gelled together as a group and soared into space?

JL: Well, it wasn't that quick. Ringo did join just as we got a recording contract, so it all really happened from then on.

TT: And when you had the feeling that you were really getting together now as a group -

JL: Yes, when he joined - after about a month, you know, we felt that it should happen now if it's going to happen at all.

TT: And was this the time that it did happen?

JL: Yes.

TT: And what is the secret in other words of this - you felt you were working together?

JL: Well I don't know what the secret was, but Ringo fitted in you know, it only took him three weeks or a month to fit in as well as the three of us had fitted in, and we'd taken years. So it was all very, very smooth after that.

TT: By 'secret' I meant - you were getting audience reaction about this time?

JL: Well we were getting audience reaction before with the other drummer we had, but we weren't satisfied. You know you can get audience reaction even if you're not - if you're playing is a bit off. No we were doing all right with the audiences, but we weren't satisfied ourselves.

TT: What's the special kind of reaction that you feel is most satisfactory to your group as such?

JL: Well, a happening or something, you know, if we're enjoying it and the music's swinging and the audience are good as well. Sometimes the audience can be very good and we're not up to standard you know. That happens to anybody, I think. When everybody's happening - we can even enjoy when we haven't got a good audience if we're really having a good session.

TT: At one of your performances last night the audience really seemed to be moving, I had this feeling and I was in it. Do you have the same - a similar reaction?

JL: Yes, but not last night because we were a bit disappointed with the microphone system, so you couldn't possibly swing in any circumstances with microphones like that. We just did our best. You know, the microphones were appalling because the audience was fairly cowered. And they would definitely have been the first audience to have heard us in the last six months. If we'd had good microphones it would have been quite interesting, but as the microphones were so bad nobody heard us. But still, the audience were all right. But they should have heard us.

TT: By 'hearing' you mean hearing the actual words?

JL: They should have heard last night - it was quiet enough to hear anything. They couldn't even hear the announcements and there was dead silence at some points when Paul was talking, and it was so distorted. Whoever set the microphones up they set the speakers right behind the microphones so every time you moved you got feedback. But tonight they're hoping to change it so if the [inaudible] is good and the microphones are good it should be - it should happen.

TT: But despite the fact that the words didn't come across there was still a fair bit of response from the audience.

JL: Oh definitely, yes, yes, but it's disappointing - you don't mind the words not coming across because the audience is so loud. Sometimes it's really you know, swinging, even if you can't hear a thing. The audience is so loud and we're so loud it's just one big noise. It's good. But last night they should have heard us, because they weren't that loud.

TT: And the screams, for example, these sounds are absolutely with you.

JL: Yes. There can be really loud screaming but you - it depends. If there's a lot of men or boys in the audience - which doesn't often

25

happen, it's only in Paris that it does - well there's no screaming, it's just sort of cheering at the end of the numbers. So you can still be quite good. Screaming is the girls' way of showing their appreciation.

TT: The sort of cheering is the male way. Roughly what proportion of male to female?

JL: Well it's 80% female on most trips, but on the Continent you tend to get equal if not more males in say Hamburg, Paris, Amsterdam, places like that. Oh yes, we've been around Europe plenty.

TT: Swinging. Did you have military training at one point?

JL: Pardon?

TT: Were you involved with military training at one point?

JL: Military training?

TT: Called up for military service?

JL: No, no nothing like that. None of us have ever been - we all missed that. I'd plan to go to some islands if they ever called me. You won't see me marching about with no hair. [laughter]

TT: Now you were saying that the audience is about 80% women 20% men. Now what different age groups do you find all over the world?

JL: Uh, 14 to 18 would be an average. On the Continent again they're older. Usually 16, 17 to 20 or over.

TT: Any idea why this might be?

JL: I don't know, because I don't think somehow this music got through at all on the Continent the way it did everywhere else. So the people of that age are only just discovering it. They missed it. Whereas the 21-22 year olds in most other places heard it when they were about 16 themselves and it passed on, you know, and they settled down, but over there I don't think they were initially there with the early Presley and all the rock'n'roll things, so I think they're sort of making up for it. And also their kids are looked after more - they're not allowed out, the 14 year olds. You won't get them out in Germany and places like that, they've got to go to bed.

TT: What - do you think they'd be the people who'd buy records though, if they're not allowed out to see you?

JL: Ah, I don't know who buys records on the Continent. It's a slow process over there. Records don't go zooming in and out. I think they'll all buy them, very slowly.

TT: So from your point of view, is it better playing to an audience or playing in a recording studio where you can't get an audience response? What difference does it make to you?

JL: Oh, well a lot of difference. You've got to be completely in tune, and completely balanced, which takes an hour or two to make records. People think that you make records with super trick equipment, but you don't. You know, you just spend more time getting a balance, which you can't do if you go to a different city each time. You've got to take pot luck on the acoustics of each hall. So when somebody complains that maybe they don't sound like the record, you know, in one town, it's 10 to 1 it's because we haven't a clue of the acoustics of the hall, and it sounds different. As for recording, it's all some shows that you do, like TV shows - not the mild ones, the good ones that take a couple of days to rehearse, and you get a good sound. And for records, you can just be perfectly in tune and balanced properly - that's why records really sound a bit different. Not that you asked me that, I thought I'd just say it.

TT: You've done an awful lot of composing of tunes, and writing of words. What are the main sort of themes that you have in mind when you get down to this, because clearly it has a tremendous impact, and an appeal to people.

JL: Well, I think a tune is the main thing, or the melody of the tune has a melody - some of them don't need one. And then it's best just to sing about love lost or love gained, as we said the other day. They're the best themes. You don't want to be singing about chairs and factories and things, leave that to the folk singers.

TT: Yes. And you in fact, and your group, have helped to move the musical tradition a stage further by the particular form of tempo that you've got at the moment, do you agree?

JL: Oh I don't know about that. I think rock'n'roll did that. Even blues did it ... you know fast blues. They sing about love. Mainly lost - the blues, but they're still singing the same basic ideas while doing fast music, about love.

TT: Who were your idols ... in your day ... more of the blues?

JL: Some of the blues artists. I didn't discover them till after I discovered rock'n'roll. Uh, Elvis Presley, Little Richard, Chuck Berry, Carl Perkins. All people, probably most people listening, will have heard of. They'll have heard of Little Richard and Elvis. The majority of people don't know Carl Perkins, for instance, who wrote 'Blue Suede Shoes' which made Elvis quite big.

TT: And were they individuals, for example?

JL: Yes, they weren't groups.

TT: They weren't groups?

JL: No, no. Later on we started liking groups. The groups we liked didn't - they weren't formed then, like The Miracles, people like that, they weren't known then. The Coasters, they're a group in America, they were out in the early days. We liked them.

TT: Is this group formation a part of the Liverpool tradition?

JL: It was, yes. When we first went to Germany and left England the first time, everybody was either Elvis Presley or Cliff Richard. They'd have a line up of the group behind, doing the dance steps, like they still do over here, all in formation ... and one fellow at the front in a gold suit. But we never played like that ... we never liked it. We always all sang and we used to wear what we liked. But we had to sort of change that a bit to get on TV and things.

TT: But on your own programme you have some of this, haven't you, some of the different suits with the first group, and there's another group that seems to be building up to the arrival of you as the main feature.

JL: Well, I don't know that - I don't know how they plan the order of appearances, they just, you know, stick us on at the end. I don't know what they do in between. I think they decide that amongst themselves and their managers. Sometimes there's a bit of a scuffle to see who goes on when, which we used to go through as well.

TT: Are there any other sort of up-and-coming groups in England or in our part of the world that ...

JL: Well England's the only place we know about really. There's quite a few up-and-coming groups, there's some good groups and they're very popular. The most popular in England at the moment, of the groups, are definitely The Rolling Stones who are entirely different from us really. People over here probably think they're like us, but they're nothing like us. They've got their own individual following and they're a very good group.

TT: Are they also from Liverpool?

JL: No, they're from London, or round about there, you know, I'm not sure. They're Southerners you know. [laughter]

TT: Are there any groups forming say in Clacton and Essex, around there?

JL: Oh yes, it's happening all the time. There's always been groups all over Britain you know, 'cos - we didn't know till we left Liverpool, but you just bump into groups. You bump into the Cliff groups, as they were, and the groups that played rock'n'roll. There were more of the Cliff and Elvis types than our type.

TT: Well, there's time for one more question, and that is: how do you manage to keep yourself intact as a human being, as a person, when all the limelight's focused on you, and what are the things you miss - what advice would you give me, for example, if I were trying to get into the limelight? What warnings would you give me? What advice about keeping myself as a person going and not being affected?

JL: I don't know - if you're affected now you're affected then, you know. There's not many people I know in this business who've suddenly become affected. If they are affected, they're affected before they start. That's all that I can say. Most of the people in this business that we've met are fairly natural. You're bound to change a bit, you know, but most of the people - the best people in this business, are natural. The ones that aren't natural and let it go to their heads are usually the ones that never really made it at all.

TT: How about some of your mates, for example, at home? Would your success be a barrier from their point of view, as well as from yours?

JL: Well the school friends that I made and, you know, you make a group of about three or four you still stick with, well I'm still in as close contact as I can be with them. And it's made no difference at all. Cos they're exactly like us, you know, so it only happens that we've got money and they haven't. And they don't care. I mean they wouldn't mind some money either.

TT: Well it's a tribute to you that you've managed to preserve this kind of relationship. Thank you very much indeed.

JL: OK goodbye.

RESULTS OF THE PSYCHOMETRIC DATA

The initial recruitment of subjects was insufficient to provide answers to the research questions, because the crowds were too packed to enable the students to move about freely and hand out invitations Perhaps in the cold light of day some of those they did approach might have had second thoughts about making a commitment to the research.

Consequently an alternative strategy for accessing subjects had to be devised. By then, having witnessed the predominance of teenagers at the airport and at a concert, and having had John Lennon confirm them as the most responsive group to Beatle music, it made sense to approach the secondary schools to recruit participants. As a result teachers from 10 schools in different socio-economic areas gladly made their classes and rooms available during lunch-breaks for the purpose, and the Principal of a Teachers College gave access to his slightly older first-year students. This time the total yield of participants was large enough to provide psychological test data from which to draw statistical conclusions.

The teachers reported many of their students to have been highly excited by the arrival of the band, but none to the point of requiring clinical referral to school medical or psychological services. From Tony's professional initial observations as the subjects filed into the testing sessions, none showed clinical signs of emotional disturbance.

But confirmation that the pool held students with the necessary range of behavioural reactions, came from a) their responses to the sound of The Beatles' music as they entered the classrooms to take the tests, b) the barracking between different groups before they settled down, and c) their acceptance or rejection of a cyclostyled set of Beatles signatures later offered as a token reward for their participation.

The respondents were separated into groups according to their scores on the now renamed *Beatle Fan Scale*. Then the 50 with the highest scores on that scale were compared with a similar number of the lowest on the set of standard measures. Then the results of a large central clump of 122 were compared with those of the groups on each

31

side. Finally the respondents were subdivided by gender to provide further inter-group comparisons on the same measures.

The outcome showed that no group recorded the psychometric features of hysteria. On the remaining measures, younger adolescent females were the most affected. Their neuroticism scale scores indicated an inclination towards emotional instability, and their scores on a major personality test were significantly higher on factors of instability, assertiveness, activity levels, worry, tension and excitability than those of their counterparts.

In turn the females in the moderate group of fans had higher scores on scales of surgency and excitability, with a tendency towards emotional instability than the group of those disinterested in The Beatles.

By comparison, the responses of the males in all groups showed far fewer departures from the broad band of stability, with only the group showing moderate enthusiasm for The Beatles being inclined significantly towards emotional instability.

Finally, the Social Background Schedule disclosed that the great majority of respondents in all groups were still living at home, with very few having been in trouble with the police.

OVERALL RESULTS

The clinical, observational and psychometric evidence was consistent in showing **no distinct psychopathology** in either the group of the keenest Beatle fans or in any other group. But the keenest fans were younger and female, and they gave psychometric indications of **developmental immaturity.** The majority of both sexes admitted they were aroused by advance publicity, the uniqueness of the occasion, the exhortations of preliminary performers, as well as the triumphal appearance of their idols. The results also suggested that inter-generational tensions combined with endemic cultural and social issues set the climate for the mass-audience response.

The findings supported psychiatrist David Ausubel's observations that girls show more emotional instability than boys, and reassuringly that the condition is mostly a transient reaction to various developmental strains. None-the-less, questions arose in Tony's mind as to whether a group of female musicians might evoke comparable reactions in young males to their music.

Tony's attention turned to the effect of the beat, not only because of the effect it had on him personally as a member of the audience, but because John Lennon had emphasised it as having opened The Beatles' route to stardom. He discussed the matter at the time with composer Jenny McLeod, later Professor of Music at Victoria University of Wellington. She confirmed that the beat frequencies of the same tunes on records as the Beatles played in concerts, varied between the extremes of 57 to 200 per minute. As for the volume, Journalist Karl du Fresne reported just recently that a technician had recorded a height of 109 decibels at one of the Wellington concerts – a level above that of a large jet-plane taking off!

It is well known that rhythm and volume affect behavior. Mothers calm the heart-beat of fractious infants by holding them close to the chest. For centuries music has also been used as a healing force. Today professional exponents of music therapy practice their skills with patients suffering a wide variety of conditions. Others have used music in association with oratory to dominate a political rally. Still others more recently to disturb the waking and sleep patterns of detainees held for interrogation.

But Tony paid rudimentary attention to the underlying psycho-physiological effects of the particular beat that The Beatles found to evoke ecstasy. Instead it focused on the immediate circumstances in which it was produced, and the characteristics of those most affected.

REFLECTIONS BASED ON THE 1964 RADIO BROADCAST when Tony Taylor made an initial attempt to describe Beatlemania

Now, what is Beatlemania, and what caused this strange, ecstatic, elated behaviour in which girls scream and men roar, and many strive to reach the front of the auditorium merely to touch their idols or to get a personal eye-wink?

Well this is a matter on which everyone has an opinion. And strangely enough, it's one of the few matters on which, although psychologists have been asked seriously for opinions, few appeared to have responded. Personally I do not incline to the view that The Beatles were equally attractive to men and women because they presented an image of the inter-sex in which neither sex was threatened. Neither, as it has also been said, do I think that they evoked feelings of motherhood in girls by making them want to cuddle them as pets. Nor do I accept the view that Beatlemania was simply the result of the manipulative methods adopted by their own business organization. Nor to my mind could it be dismissed solely as the musical fad of the younger generation.

Granted that there was a constant and increasing warning of pending disruption in the news media in advance of the Beatles' arrival, and that their image and commercial successes were in focus for months before the group arrived here in New Zealand. But in my opinion Beatlemania would have arisen without that build-up, i.e. if people had just come to see and hear them out of curiosity. Admittedly without the publicity The Beatles would not have attracted 30,000 people in six days in New Zealand. Technicians might also have been primed the audiences with screams piped in from the vast array of loudspeakers on the stage: but as far as I could tell there were no artificial screams nor paid screamers to stimulate gatherings at the airport.

What then is Beatlemania? I haven't enough facts to go on at the moment, but soon I hope to be in a better position to determine whether the screamers are as different from the 'normals' as many people declare. Until those factual results are to hand, perhaps I too can indulge in flights of opinion about Beatlemania, just like everyone else.

The Beatles stand on the balcony of the St George Hotel, Wellington

I begin by assuming that the screamers are not very different from 'normals'. Therefore instead of looking for an explanation in terms of individual eccentricity or psychopathology, as many commentators are wont to do, here I shall consider the opposite – the effect of music on groups composed of ordinary individuals. In the Middle Ages such people danced in groups in a desperate attempt to keep the recurrent Black Death plague at bay. Some observers regarded such behavior as futile and attributed it simply to the effects of eating ergot fungus in rye. Unlike them, physician/polymath Paracelcus ascribed the condition to 'the blood (*being*) set in commotion in consequence of an alteration in the vital spirits, whereby fits of intoxicating joy and the propensity to dance are occasioned' (cf. http://www.public-domaincontent.com/books/black_death_dancing_mania/d15.shtml - accessed 20 June 2014). He seemed to be on the right track, although for many of the dancers the 'joy' became a compulsion unto death.

Listen to excerpts from the Nuremberg mass-rallies of the 1930s and 1940s in which music and demagoguery were used to foster belligerence and militarism. (See Michael O'Leary's novel *Magic Alex's Revenge* ((ESAW, 2008)) which contrasts the Nazis' 'All You

Need is Hate' philosophy, with that of The Beatles' 'All You Need is Love').

Mass-audience reaction is most certainly a topic worthy of detailed study. In the meantime, one could do worse than adopt the definition provided by lugubrious lawyer and Vice-Chancellor of Victoria University Jim Williams in 1964 that 'Beatlemania is the reaction of some young people in excess of that which others might consider appropriate in the circumstances'!

REQUIEM

Flip Side of the Ballad of John and Yoko
Written after the 6pm News, Tuesday, Ninth of December, 1980

"
E

We have just heard from New York
ex-Beatle John Lennon was shot today . . . !!!!!!"

i
There I was sitting on a sofa
In one of the southernmost cities of the world
Listening to the radio whilst thinking about cooking tea

Well, how can you be honest about how you feel?

I'd just turned the station over
To get the "real" news of the world
When I heard the words written above: well fuck me!

What else can you do but swear at a time like this

I am thinking about my mother, his mother
Two of the responsible for bringing us into the world
And now John, you're gone! There's only me

Yoko and me, and the rest of humanity together in grief and love

Yoko's in a black scumbag, I left the sofa
Wandered aimlessly around the room the day you left the world
Your death is a climax of events forcing mortality on me

Everybody's talkin' 'bout Pol Pot, Nazism, Socialism, I.R.A. and junkies

Give me a chance, brother
You have helped me understand this world
Now you're dead, am I enslaved or freeeeeeeeeeeeee!!!!!!!!!

Fuck the revolution, we have bred another generation

                              ii
When it all began, I was just another
Beatle fan. A teenager from the other side of the world
Looking for something more interesting than school's authority

Distances traveled in space, time and sorrow add up to one thing

Your songs and books helped me discover
In myself, what all the education in the world
Could not; that I could write and illustrate my own story

Knowledge to one is ignorance to another, unless there is love

1968, Hey Jude, the death of my father and mother
Like a lost black sheep I entered the outside world
Sold my records, went to work in a dark, thankless factory

If a person makes enough of one thing, he or she becomes a thing

While I got lost in nothing, you found your lover
For whom you left the Beatles, left the wife, shocked the world
Yoko, through the years of illusion, offered you reality

Eternity may be a stone in Wales, but it is now we must live

And so, lest the press smother
You and your love, both withdrew from the world
Which had built you a boat of fame, then left you all at sea

How many oak trees have been allowed to grow from the acorns?

"Just like starting over"
Is not starting over, you are now dead to the world
Sean and Yoko no longer have the shade and strength of their tree

That fallen tree made them a house which they must make a home

                    iii
We were always a decade away from each other
Yet we were of the same generation
You were the spiritual pathfinder
I followed to the point of penetration
And I never lost you, but let you go

It was not lack of love, but life itself, caused the separation

Now you too have joined the dead and living dead
Who haunt and torment my existence
On this quaint and sadly crazy planet on which
To live is not just to breath, but an insistence
That each such breath is a test of courage and will

Which we understand at a metaphorical distance

Christl
         I know
                    It ain't easy!

                                        Michael O'Leary 1980

The Pataka Māori group welcomes the group from Liverpool

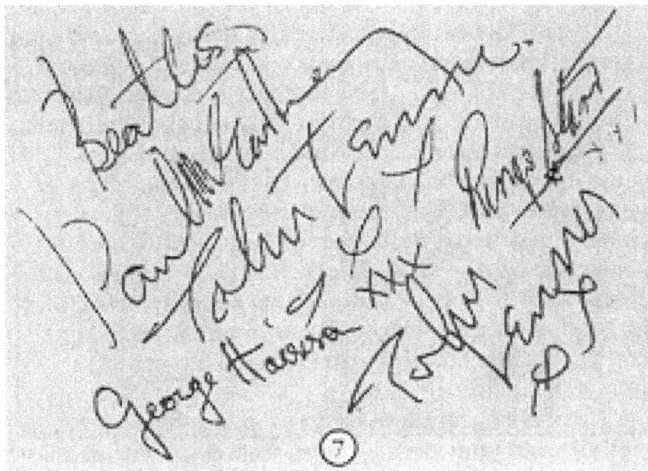

And in the end, the love you take
Is equal to the love you make.
(*The End*: Lennon/McCartney from The Beatles'
final 1969 'Abbey Road' album).

John Lennon's New Zealand connections

John Lennon with his New Zealand cousins from Levin

As well as the cousins above John Lennon's New Zealand family included his second cousin, Upper Hutt resident Lynda Mathews. She grew up reading about her English cousin in letters, and got to meet him for the first time in Wellington's St George Hotel (below).

John Lennon very nearly came to live in New Zealand as a six year old when his father, Freddy, planned to emigrate here with his son. The plan was thwarted by John's Aunt Mimi - she alerted John's mother, Julia, who stopped it.

www.ingramcontent.com/pod-product-compliance
Lightning Source LLC
Chambersburg PA
CBHW060639030426
42337CB00018B/3401